A Grain of Sand

Why we are here, and Who we are

Understanding Our Universal Consciousness

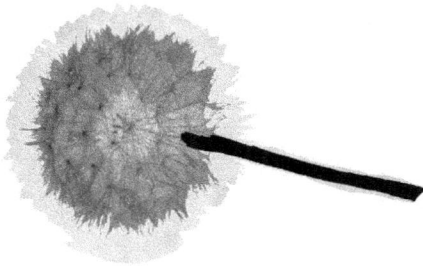

by

Paul Manuel

Published in Canada 2015

ISBN: 978-0-9918393-0-8

Cover art by Alexandra Manuel
Special thanks to Hubble STScI for use of galaxy image.
Typeset in *Baskerville* at SpicaBookDesign

Printed with www.createspace.com

THE GRAIN OF SAND

I AM THE GRAIN OF SAND
IN WHICH ETERNITY IS REVEALED

I AM ETERNITY
IN WHICH THE GRAIN OF SAND
IS MANIFEST

I AM ALWAYS
I AM ALL

I AM CREATION
I AM CREATOR

I AM

TABLE OF CONTENTS

INTRODUCTION

Why did I write this book?

First of all I would like to thank you for taking the time to look into this book. My hope is that it will entertain and inspire.

It is a compilation of my poetry and my understanding of our complete eternal nature, (the material, spiritual and non-judgemental aspects of our being.) I do my best to convey what I know as clearly as I am able. I have answered questions concerning our nature as I know them to be. I do not go into minute details of our every experience, because it is not necessary. When we understand the big picture, everything else becomes more understandable.

When concise descriptive terminology fails, I have used poetry to stir emotions, which I hope will stimulate deeper understanding.

As you may know, there is wisdom in all things.

My wish is that my poetry and philosophy will help people to realize that we must change the way we interact with each other, and our wonderful planet. Of course we need not change everything about ourselves. We are essentially good beings. Our ability to love just needs to be boosted a bit to include "all things."

When love becomes our basic intention as beings, amazing things will happen. We will have opened the door to a new reality, a reality of peace. My intention is to help make this world a safe place for everyone.

I see a world without fear. A world where everyone is aware of their divinity.

The main focus of this book is to inspire a clearer understanding of our complete nature, so that our current manifestation is no longer run by a purely egotistic mandate, but from our divinity state.

It is now time, we are entering a New Age. The age of Spiritual Enlightenment.

Paul Manuel

PREFACE

Hopefully you will find this book inspiring or at the very least interesting.

That being said, everyone will interpret this book in their own way.

Whether I'm right, or whether I'm wrong is for you to decide.

As long as you start your spiritual journey, that is the main thing. The absolute truth that we are the infinite being, without beginning, without end, will come to you.

I have spent years pondering these questions and have realized the profound truth of our being, it was never completely hidden, just masked.

We are all aware of our divinity to some degree because it is a part of our complete identity. This may be difficult to believe because of circumstances, but if we keep asking the truth will be revealed.

That you and I have come together at this moment is the result of your intention to become aware of your complete being. Your divinity is responding to your intention.

Why we are here and who we are

Why we are here: We are universal intelligence, manifested in this reality with its parameters so as to experience possibilities. Not unlike an artist experimenting with different media and different concepts.

Who we are: We are divine beings. We are a focal point of the Universal Intelligence.

Why doesn't everyone know this fact intuitively? Because that would compromise this physical experience. To experience this physical reality in the purest possible way we have set parameters in place to mask our complete identity. But it is not blocked 100% it is just beneath the surface. The awareness of our complete identity becomes clearer upon the intention to become aware of it.

Time to Awaken

We were manifested in this manner to experience this reality without prior knowledge of our spiritual nature. We started with innocence and no knowledge of our non-material reality so that we would have no distractions from our physical experience.

We wanted to immerse ourselves in this reality. We wanted to have it without prejudices. We wanted to experience it as the only reality and that is what we have done. We created this physical experience in the best possible way.

That being said, sooner or later the blockers had to break down and that is what's happening now. We no longer accept reality as purely physical. We are resonating on more than one level. We are beginning to feel a profound connection to others, not just our species but all species, all things.

We are awakening, not as from a dream, but metaphorically as in *Becoming Aware* of our complete nature.

Immortality

I can remember as a youth lying in my bed thinking about what I was, questioning my reality.

I remember thinking "What is this conversation I'm having in my head, and who I am having it with?" From where does it spring, this conversation, this concept of being more than my physical being? I came to the realization that I had no boundaries, I was an endless manifestation.

I was in fact the origin of the question and the answer, I felt absolutely as an immortal. I experienced infinite reality. I knew I could never cease to be.

It is not uncommon for people to have feelings of immortality because it is the truth. You can die, but you cannot cease to be.

I Am

I am within
I am without
I am a whisper
I am a shout

I am what I think I am
I am so much more

I am here
I am there
I am everywhere

I am nowhere to measure
I am the measure of all

I am winter
I am spring
I am summer
I am fall

I am anything
I am everything
I am big
I am small

One thing I cannot be
Is nothing at all

The Ego

We gave ourselves a survival mechanism, it is our Ego. To exist is its prime directive.

We are designed to exist in this physical reality with its parameters. The ego is the governing force of this manifestation, it is extremely powerful within the material realm. To all intents and purposes this reality is "everything" to the ego, and as such it is most comfortable with the one reality mentality.

As a species, our egoic sense of self has us firmly entrenched in this physical reality and that can make it very difficult for some people to become aware of their spiritual nature.

But this is changing.

We are a Manifestation

From Intention of Universal Intelligence

To experience Possibilities

Seeking

In a crowd of one
My senses reel
A tossed salad of voices
Each with mixed emotions
A vortex of eddies
Scrambling for recognition
Unable to focus
Voices of chaos

Swirling, senseless chatter
Confusion in motion
Seeking
Ever seeking
Out of sync
Anchor lost
Adrift in raging seas

A bubble
In wind tossed foam
Bursting, reforming
Seeking
Ever seeking

Paul Manuel

A membrane
Between vacant thoughts
Stretching, bursting
To cringe
In the presence of the uninvited

Unborn possibilities
Cascading
Clarity without form
Then silence
Calm
Being without judgement
Without expectation
Just being
At peace

The ego is an urge, a rule, a plan or mandate

It is not a separate entity, but it can seem like one because it is always referred to as separate. It is a survival mechanism that can give an overwhelming urge to react.

When we open our mind to our complete being our ego may cause us to shrink back in fear because it is confronted with the unknown or what is considered the unknowable, and when the ego feels threatened, it must react. That reaction can manifest as denial or something will come up and our train of thought will change.

With continued meditation the unknown will become the known and the egoic influence of denial will diminish.

I am all things

Ever present, ever potent

Everything to do with this material existence is favorable to the ego

Everything to do with this material existence is favorable to the ego, except the true pursuit of spiritual enlightenment. Procreative desires, hoarding and the pursuit of power, all to do with survival are acceptable.

Metaphorically, it says, I will go over the hill to the next village and I will do whatever it takes including killing if necessary, so that I can have what they have and I and my village will have a greater chance of survival. We release ourselves from our egoic control when we view this physical reality from the spiritual prospective.

The ego is non-thinking, it is a feeling that makes us react.

You must remember the ego is only in control as long as you allow it.

We need to step back as it were, which allows the realization that we are more than the sum of our parts. We have the ability to do this abstract exercise, we are spiritual. At this point we will be in a position to realize that this is just that, an experience to participate in possibilities, this is our adventure and as such is controlled by our intention and that will give us the strength or the insight to change the circumstances of our experience.

Your spirit and the ego

You have the ability to analyze yourself. Question yourself. No other being on this planet to my knowledge can do this!

Because you are a conscious being and capable of spiritual awareness, you can change your egoic mandate. You can take away the ego's power to some degree allowing a more favorable balance. It may take some time, or it may happen quickly, but it will happen, if that is your intention.

Question: Is the ego the body's desires?

Answer: It influences through desire which is manifested through actions of the mind and physical body. It is your survival mechanism.

Question: Why do our emotions seem to come from the physical body?

Answer: Because emotions reveal themselves most vividly within our physical frame. This is not to say emotions are strictly physical. Emotions are also experienced psychologically there is no divisive point. This is not so obvious to some people only because their emotions are experienced more concretely within their physical frame.

Explanation using computers as metaphor

It is like saying a program is the computer. The program is not the computer. There are many components to a computer and they must interact as a whole to function. We are not so different. Our complete nature is indivisible from our experiences holistically speaking.

Our ego influences our thinking and our emotions which result in judgment or a knee-jerk reaction, it can influence us psychologically or physiologically, whatever is necessary for survival.

We have become far too capable

In my opinion: We are existing in a very dangerous climate because we have become far too capable to **allow a primeval egoic instinctive mandate to run our experience.**

As human beings we are inquisitive and as a result, we are becoming aware of our universal consciousness which changes our reality. This physical reality is a reality of inter-action, opinion and judgment. With a less egoic approach we will make much more intelligent decisions instead of knee-jerking along. We can make the decisions that will enhance our experience in a harmonious fashion, where all things are realized as equal, where respect and love are paramount.

We are moving into an enlightened age!

The ego is trying to control our priorities

Our egoic mandate is trying to keep us focused on our earthly instinctive nature. *We*, are trying our best to overcome our instinctive nature.

As a result, there is conflict. In order for us to advance, our ego has to be changed. Its mandate has to be re-thought. It is still there, but we need to change its priorities, and that is what's happening.

In fact this is our survival mechanism working, it is evolution in progress!

Farewell

Why do I covet
What cannot be?
What force in my nature
I cannot see?

Yet something compels
Driving me on
Can desire
For desires sake
Be right, or be wrong?

I find
Behind desire
When desire controls
A prompting from something
Ageless, yet old

Smoke within smoke
A wisp of suggestion
Caressing demanding
Directing, directing

As I face my desire
It retreats to its lair
It is ego hidden
Hidden, but there

Paul Manuel

I sense
I am aware
I see with mind's eye

Ah yes
There you are
Ancient, so ancient

I need you no longer
Old friend
Though you try
To hunger me still

I bid you farewell
In others you will thrive
Passing along
As they open mind's eye

I soar now anew
Blessed with clear vision
Free from illusion

The strongest
And weakest
Of prisons

The Non-Judgemental Infinite Eternal Universe

What we think can manifest a sympathetic reality to that intention. Either now in our immediate reality, or in the next manifestation or reality (as in after death). It is not because the infinite reality cares, *it doesn't*.

Question: Why would a non-judgmental universal intelligence manifest anything, if it doesn't care, if it doesn't have personality, or if it is unaware?

Answer: Because manifestation is the result of *our* desire. The physical, spiritual and non-judgemental aspects of our nature have an indivisible relationship. We are in fact one, and the same. We desire, and our non-judgemental realm of unlimited potential manifests that desire, that is all.

An example of this one-ness is that it is not unlike the mind. The conscious aspect of the mind desires, the sub-conscious aspect of the mind is affected by that desire. The conscious and sub-conscious are indivisible.

Our divinity will be revealed to us if it is our intention to become aware of it. We are in fact indivisible from our divinity. There will come a moment (usually through meditation) when we realize this as the absolute truth. In that moment we will have remembered our holistic identity. It is an amazing enlightenment and it is not complicated. It just is.

It is not difficult, in fact for some people, this realization comes in a flash, with apparently no conscious intention. It is not difficult, again, it just is.

I've decided at this time to explain what spiritual enlightenment is, because it can be so misunderstood.

I have spoken to numerous people over the years about this subject. There were those who believed that a spiritually enlightened being must radiate enlightenment, as described by so many religions and mythologies. To glow or levitate, display the classic heavenly presence or god-like abilities. I believe this is possible, but it is certainly not necessary. There are degrees of enlightenment. It is like a dimmer switch: the bulb is "on" from dim to bright, but it is on! Understanding enlightenment from the "off" position is difficult, because we are in the dark and we tend to rely on traditional descriptions of enlightenment which may be misleading.

If you are searching for the awareness of your complete identity, you have turned on the "light". The mere act of asking or seeking, is spiritual enlightenment.

Step Into the Light

What face do I see
always looking,
looking back at me?
Laughter lines
Etched in stone
Sorrows, darkness
Born alone
Pleading to be understood
Deep within its hood.

Face aglow
With inner light
Eyes clear free and bright
By what sight
Do these eyes see?
These eyes so bright
Clear and free

These eyes, these eyes
All are me
Dark and hooded
Bold and free
These eyes
A Window
Through the mask
Revealing now, future, past

Paul Manuel

A mix and mingle
Truth and lies
My spirit walks
It crawls, it flies
All is seen
In mine own eyes

All is seen
In kindred eye
Truth, illusion, lies
All behind the eyes

Eyes the windows of the soul
Wisdom, Wisdom
From days of old
Ancient story
Retold

Just the trials
And tribulations
Of universal participation
Seeking, seeking
Living life without the chains
Without the pain
Of inner strife.

To iron out the wrinkles
No hidden cache of doubt
To throw the hood of darkness
Step into the Light

Intention

Intention creates a reality sympathetic to the energy of that intention.

The universal manifesting aspect of our reality responds to desire, whether conscious or sub-conscious. It will respond to positive or negative energy, meaning beneficial or non-beneficial intention to our situation without prejudice. It responds to the energy of desire, not the content.

What we think, how we live, what our "true" feelings are, will manifest a sympathetic reality in our immediate manifestation or the next (as in after death). Not because the infinite cares, it doesn't. What you manifest is a result of the energy you direct to the non-judgmental. It is what I would term a Karmic response.

You need to be aware of who and what you are in order to realize a reality that will be harmonious to your desires; a reality that you will be content with. This can be attained through meditation.

That being said, there are those of us that are living a life of peace, love, compassion and empathy; they are responding to their divinity, not necessarily aware of it, and as such will also realize a sympathetic reality to that energy.

Coarse Energy

What ever your dominant energy is, whether good or evil coarse or fine, will manifest a reality sympathetic to that energy.

Coarse Energy (negative thoughts of purely material orientation) held in check is not the dominant energy, what is holding it in check is the dominant energy.

Coarse Energy need not be feared as an inevitable path to an unwanted reality, but it must be *acknowledged because it can and will influence possibilities.*

Through acknowledgment, coarse energy diminishes, having less and less influence.

**Death is a transition state, you will attract a reality
which supports your energy signature.
It is up to you (personally.)**

In Death you will attract a reality that supports what your
energy signature favors, without prejudice.

You can branch off into a similar reality, comparable to the
one we now experience . Or depending upon the frequency
of your energy, you will attract in varying degrees a darker or
brighter reality.

In other words, a person with evil thoughts, intentions and
actions, will manifest in varying degrees into a reality that
will support that energy. Equally dark or darker

The opposite is true for a person with peaceful and loving
energy. In death they will manifest in varying degrees, into
an equally loving or brighter and more enlightened reality.

The realm of unlimited potential does not care one way or
the other, it is without judgment or opinion. It is responding
to your personal energy signature.

There is an old saying "You reap what you sow."

Paul Manuel

We have to start new and let the past go

The answer lies in forgiveness. When we cease to dwell upon what has been, we will be free to step into a new reality. We need to forgive our past transgressions and that will lead to peace and harmony.

With forgiveness, our priorities change. We will become more thoughtful of what we are doing and how it affects everything around us. We will deal with what needs to be dealt with then move on.

What do we really need? We need to understand that we are divine beings and accept ourselves as one with all, we are indivisible from reality which includes everything. Once we realize our complete nature which is physical, spiritual and non-judgemental, this conclusion becomes unavoidable.

One of Many Truths

When you have realized your divinity,
there will always be forgiveness

When you find divinity
You find forgiveness
When you find forgiveness
You find peace.

New Beginning

Dwell not
Upon the future
Nor what the past has stored
Now is calm between these storms
Be now in the state of calm
A state sublime without demand
Where divinity is unimpaired

Be at peace
In the joy of knowing, not knowing
Without judgement
Without expectation

Rest
Where the soul resides
In infinite bliss
Apart from the vibrations of intention

On returning
Allow intention to begin afresh
With deeper understanding
Unfettered by distress

Freedom Found

We are universal intelligence
Experiencing possibilities

When all is said and done
We interact to experience
Each and everyone

To seek the light
Doesn't mean
Putting life on hold
It doesn't mean
Giving up
Letting love grow cold

It means to see
With inner eye
The miracle of being
To know
That we are infinite
Therein to find
True freedom

Our ego has worked well for us up to now

Here we are, this rather delicate, thin-skinned creature which cannot run very fast, cannot do anything physically defensive compared to other predators pound for pound, a naked human is pretty defenseless. But we are smart. We can extrapolate possibilities. Some other animals do so as well. They can plan ahead and hunt for prey, in a limited fashion, as the moment dictates. But we can plan years ahead! We can imagine hundreds of different possibilities, and because of that when we are hungry we create ways to satisfy that hunger.

When we need to defend ourselves we create ways to become more powerful. We invent tools and weapons or diplomacy. We take advantage however and wherever possible.

This is the survival mechanism at work: Some people hoard money, food, effort of other people. Hoarding things that are intangible. Collection of information can be part of the process of survival. The pursuit of power, whom ever is the most powerful has the best chance of survival.

Some people have reached a point where they are very powerful on this planet. It has been a process of trial and elimination where they have taken advantage of every opportunity to empower themselves. It doesn't matter how it affects humanity or the environment, because from an egoic standpoint it is survival of the fittest, perfectly acceptable behavior. But their survival mechanism is out of sync with current reality. Their behavior and our behavior must change because it is threatening our survival. And that is precisely what is happening at this time.

Where there is opportunity, there is someone to take advantage. A king or queen perhaps, the link between the Gods and the people, there are many hats that would improve his or her chances of survival.

Because certain things seem to increase our chances of survival, our egos have latched on to these people also as a survival technique. Because if we no longer have to face the unknown individually, we can get on with life, letting someone else take the risks and responsibility. This increases our sense of security.

But this behavior has gotten out of control on both levels. We need leaders, not dictators, participants, not sheep. We can change our singular and collective nature if we so choose.

This is **an interactive experience**.

I am King

Hiding in the efforts of others
Deep within
Material wealth
Comforted
By the things of man
I am surrounded
By creations of art
Only I
And few others
Can amass

I grow weary
At times
With my possessions
They have no warmth
Only luster

I am locked
With chains of desire
Stronger than chains
Of iron
To these possessions
And still I covet
With an insatiable desire
To possess

I would that I could
Relinquish all
For a true friend
Or true love

But I have no power
To surrender
I have been captured
I am imprisoned

Paul Manuel

Within the confines of time
Within the physically tangible
Within Desire

Do not speak to me
Of ethereal things
It is illusion of which you speak
Daydreams of those
Who have naught to lose
But I
I have everything
That money can buy
I do not cry for want

I have power
It is within my grasp
To control the lives of others
Do I not have everything?

I am fulfilling my desires
I covet only because I can
Only a few can boast as I
And if I tire at times
It is only weakness
It will pass
It always does

I can buy distractions
I can buy love
But not true love
The poorest of the poor
Have what I have not
True love
But then I have the money
And the pain

Leave me now
I am King

The physical, spiritual and the non-judgemental realities

The physical reality is the judgmental reality, and we are the awareness of the Universe that makes judgment.

The spiritual is an ethereal reality, it is also judgemental but with greater understanding.

The non-judgemental is the calm in deep meditation. It is the realm of no opinion. It is also the realm of unlimited potential.

There are different aspects of our holistic identity, but there is only one existence and that includes everything.

The knowledge of this is masked by different degrees of awareness, but there is no absolute separation point.

The physical, spiritual and non-judgemental realities are in essence indivisible and **this is our complete nature**.

We are, the Universal Judgment

The awareness of being is the state of judgment. We are beings of judgment.

We, as beings, are the consciousness of existence.

The non-judgmental is the realm of unlimited potential without opinion, it just is. It is beyond sense of being or identity, therefore no judgments.

Only we, as beings, not only human but beings of every description, have concerns about our reality individually or collectively.

Consciousness, is a divine state sometimes lost in the moment, but it is never absent.

If you question your identity and seek to understand your complete nature, you beckon divinity. You will realize at some point that you are a divine being. At this point you will understand the physical state, the spiritual state and the state of unlimited potential as indivisible, as a truth. This is enlightenment.

Our Spiritual Complete Nature and the Ego

Our spiritual complete nature is: the physical, the spiritual and the non-judgemental, remember, there is no divisive point. And as such the ego is part of our nature. But we have the ability to become aware of the egoic influence for what it is, and that awareness will change the way we interact with each other and reality as a whole.

Stepping Out or Waking Up as part of the Collective

We are infinite eternal beings manifested within the parameters of time and space, experiencing possibilities. The awareness of our complete nature has been masked so that we would have the opportunity to experience this physical reality in the purest possible way with independence and free choice.

That being said, everybody has a sense of the spiritual reality. We manifested from the constant......to the constant change reality. The **constant** is the changeless, timeless and the formless. The **constant change** reality is our physical and spiritual reality. We are inseparable from these realities because they are indivisible and as a result, everyone has a sense of their spirituality but not everyone acknowledges or believes it. A global awakening is now beginning, it is the natural order of things, it may take a while, but it cannot be stopped.

The socialism that is in a healthy family unit is spreading out to incorporate all of mankind, which will lead to the realization that in reality all things are indeed family.

As soon as we step out of our material parameters, our infinite nature opens up to us because we are infinite beings.

Awakened

Standing on a street corner
I am wine in paper bag
Blinded by prism vision
I am in the vapor of time
Circling in an eddy of despair
Lost

A thought fills my being
In a moment
I am blessed with vision
I rush forward
I am a current
In the ocean of infinity

Touched with divine understanding
Only touched
Yet I am filled
With love and peace

The brilliance of this moment
Will fade
But it can never
Flicker and die

I have touched eternity
I have awakened

Paul Manuel

Spirituality can be a threat to the Ego

Some people have a need to be *told* the way it is about spirituality. They like the idea of spirituality, but it is a mystery best left for others to solve.

This is perfect for our ego because now we do not have to deal with the unknown. Now the ego is not threatened by spirituality, because we are not focusing our attention on our spiritual nature. We are just accepting the rhetoric of the written word, which unfortunately has been used in many cases to inhibit rather than enhance clear thought or awareness of our complete nature.

The Ego can put up blockers when we attempt to understand our spirituality:
It can seem threatening to our sense of self or self-importance

Our Ego can put up blockers to discourage us from asking certain questions. The ego is not a separate entity, it is an urge or suggestive force. It is a survival mechanism.

Intellectualizing the possibility of spirituality is not an enlightened awareness of spirituality, but it is a threat to our ego because we are contemplating the unknown or unknowable.

There are people who can only intellectualize that we are infinite beings, because the awareness of this knowledge as a truth, from an egoic stand-point is not possible. It can threaten our sense of self and self-importance. Our egoic response to the pursuit of this awareness is to say: "We will delve into the unknown intellectually." "We will go so far as to analyze this unknown with available information, but we will stop there. Because really it's just a bunch of nonsense." Then we can put the pursuit of spiritual awareness aside, and our sense of self-importance is re-established as most important and we can get on with the business of survival.

These people do not really believe in their spirituality.

The fear of deity judgement, which is a result of the rhetoric they have been subjected to throughout their life, is something better left for others to contemplate. They would rather accept what they have been told or assume that death is final, than to take responsibility for their personal spiritual journey.

The truth is, what we harbor within ourselves: love, compassion, forgiveness or the opposites: hate, indifference, resentment, create vibrations of intention that will manifest a sympathetic reality in the hereafter and that may be construed as Karmic judgement.

Once we realize within our egoic self that the pursuit of our divinity is not a threat, but that it is **a powerful asset to our existence**, our egoic mandate will change to support rather than hinder our advancing consciousness towards spiritual awakening.

The thing is, when we really become aware of our holistic identity, we realize the business of our personal survival must include the survival of everything else. We are less controlled by our egoic nature and we begin **to consider the welfare of others** *as important as our own.*

This awakening is a perspective change that is bringing us into a new age.

Without End

I am the door
I seek to open
I alone
Am the key

I am the truth
I am a beacon
I need not eyes
To see

Hinges rusty
Bolt is seized
Door is old
And stuck

But the door
Is just a figment
Floating
Not real
Just rhetoric

I am the light
I am the glory
As is everything

I am
And always have been
Without beginning
Without end

Paul Manuel

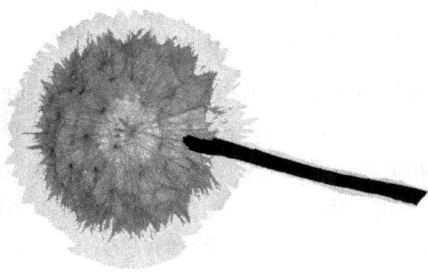

The beginning of spiritual enlightenment

There comes a time in everyone's life, during this physical manifestation or another, when we begin to see a greater reality and strive to understand how we fit within it. This is the beginning of our spiritual enlightenment. There will be something in us driving us on. This is our awareness seeking truth and this allows our infinite consciousness to breach the barriers of our physical reality leading to our enlightenment.

But the ego has a seemingly unlimited reservoir of ammunition to block Enlightenment in some people.

I need to clarify this. The ego will try to protect you from going into the unknown. That is its job.

For some people, it will consider them delving into spirituality as a threat (it is the unknown). It will throw things at you *that you're familiar with*. It will present what you would consider rational objections. They are a product of your physical reality, and as such are very effective distractions.

The truth is that you are an infinite being, the awareness of this truth lies just beneath these layers of rhetoric that have been your life experiences. For some people it can be hard to put these distractions aside.

What you have to do is understand the rhetoric for what it is. It is your past experiences coupled with speculation. To accept this as truth you must learn to view physical reality from the infinite perspective. This will result in the realization that you have always been doing your best utilizing available information. There is no blame, there is no argument, it is just memory and it cannot be changed. But it can be understood for what it is.

The rhetoric will not disappear, but it will no longer have as strong an influence.

The Proverbial Door

To open the door of the mind
To expose the infinite truth
May seem hard
And ever resistant
Barring from finding the proof

That the feeling of being forever
Is not just a fanciful dream
But that I am an eternal being
A being with no beginning no end

That I am timeless
I am formless
I am more than meets the eye
That the door I seek to open
Is a figment, nothing more

That now
Is the origin of moment
Moment the beginning of time

Time is a tool of the physical
Time is a tool
Nothing more

Time is what masks
The infinite being
Time
The Proverbial Door

Paul Manuel

When you understand our physical reality as a constant change yet infinite reality

You will become aware of the infinite reality without form or parameters which is also real. You will realize that you are in fact inseparable from these realities because you are all of reality.

Layers and layers of experiences which I consider to be baggage can make it difficult to realize the truth of our complete being. But we don't have to peel away the layers. It is just rhetoric within our minds. These are things that happened in our physical experience. They are just memories but they are real because they do exist and as a result they can negatively or positively affect the realization of our complete nature. What we must do is view our memories as a localized event at which point we will have accessed the spiritual reality which leads to awareness of the reality of unlimited potential, which is the reality without form without judgement, a reality of complete peace. Bliss.

I know it may seem difficult, but it will happen. It is experienced as a flash of profound clarity, you will have touched eternity, and at this point you will understand this physical reality for what it is. **It is only a part of our complete holistic identity.**

Another method is that you can view memories like the layers of an onion and some people need to do this

A good thing to know about peeling an onion is that you may cry if you do not peel it carefully. There may be terrible memories and long established habits that you are trying to get through and it can be painful. But there will come a moment when you will suddenly find yourself apart from this confusion of rhetoric and see it for what it is and how it influences you.

This can be achieved through meditation. Of course we are all unique and for some people going through the layers will be more difficult than for others. That is how it must be, but the end result will be the same. Spiritual enlightenment cannot be stopped.

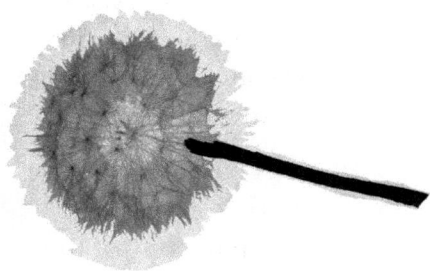

Motion of the Soul

Motion of the Soul
Music to the ear
Music is poetry
For all the world to hear

The rhythm of the spirit
Released to soar on high
No question, no answer
Just being
Here and now

Play the strings of passion
Whatever they may be
To play your music openly
Is truly to be free

A balance
A true oneness
With the harmony of life
Beyond the pain and suffering
Of anxiety and strife

Paul Manuel

To flow
With cosmic glory
To be a living light
An instrument
Within an instrument
In a moonlit
Subtle night

A snowy landscape
Sparkled crust
A crackle
Crisp and clean
Only joy
No truth, no lies
Just smiles and tears
And pounding heart

No thought, no cost, no toll
Just peace
And harmony
In the motion of the soul

The ego utilizes past experiences to entrench us in the physical reality

The ego utilizes past experiences to entrench us in this physical reality. Our guilt, fear, hate and desire are readily available ammunition for the ego. They are very powerful mechanisms in this physical reality.

If stepping out all at once seems impossible, it is because there are too many distractions, you just need to keep trying and these distractions will fade. Keep asking questions. "What am I?" "Who am I?" At some point in your meditations your complete nature will be revealed. The realization of our complete nature is there for the asking. It cannot be blocked 100%, it is just beneath the surface. When it is revealed it is in a flash of profound undeniable clarity, there is no buildup it just happens.

As a more enlightened being, forgiving ourselves and others becomes not only easier but unavoidable. Understanding from our divinity state is understanding these emotions for what they are, thus removing much of their power. Condemn the deed not the doer becomes clearly understood. This does not mean we idly stand by and allow evil to run amuck, it means that we have greater understanding of what it is. And as a result we can now deal with it in a calmer enlightened fashion rather than as a knee-jerk reaction.

The Universe is curious,

and we fulfill that curiosity.

This is our purpose.

This is our nature.

A Simple Question

The reflection of life
In the water
Speaks to me
Of things unseen
I ask why
What is the answer?
Am I just a reflection
Of all that I have been?

As I ponder
A fish breaks the mountain
Again
Then again and again
The mountain breaks into ripples
Distortions, reflections
The same

Oh why?
What is the answer
That hides
Behind the disguise?
So many reflections
Cloud my vision
The vision
Of what I am

Sometimes I'm near
My vision is clear
I sense the greater truth

Then come the lies
Of reflections
Distortions of life
I have learned
And I am lost
In the ripples of distractions
The reflection
Of all that I have been

Riddles
Puzzles
Illusions

Distractions
Reflections
Lies

So many distortions
In place to deceive
It's amazing I know I'm alive
Yet
I sense truth of being
Of being
Outside of time

Envision a balloon

You are living inside of this balloon. The skin of the balloon is the perimeter of your reality. This balloon can be a tiny localized event or it can encompass the known universe. No matter how vast this balloon becomes it is still a contained reality. And a contained reality no matter how vast, is a localized event when viewed from the infinite perspective.

We, being infinite eternal beings, have the ability to realize this as the absolute truth. We are all of reality and as such are only limited by our desire or interest to become aware of our complete nature.

About Reality

Reality is the physical reality, the spiritual reality and the non-judgemental reality.
The non-judgemental reality is the realm of unlimited potential.

These seemingly independent realities are in truth indivisible.

We, being a part of reality, are indivisible from all aspects of reality. We are in fact infinite and eternal.

We are eternity experiencing self.
We are the eternal being.

We are a Manifestation from the Intention of the Universal Intelligence to Experience Possibilities.

I would like to say at this time that people have a tendency to believe that they cannot influence the state of the environment without physical activity. That is not true. We are the environment, we are all connected. This is an interactive experience, and as such responds to our intention.

Every action has a reaction whether it is a vocal, physical or a mental action. If your intention is to change something on any one of these levels your intention will be realized to a greater or lesser degree. Recently there has been a desire for change in the way we interact socially as a species as well as how we interact with our environment. That intention has manifested the beginnings of a paradigm shift, which is the only way this desire can be realized.

I do know that history is full of failed wishes and dreams. Sometimes in the moment the intentions of the few outweight the wishes and dreams of the many for good or for bad. Horrific things are happening at this very moment to someone or something somewhere and that is our disgrace. But the only way to stop this behavior is a paradigm shift. You could say it is long overdue, but things are as they are. What they will or can be is up to us.

There are those that will support the shift and those that will oppose it, which is their choice. But opposing the paradigm shift can only hinder what cannot be stopped. This paradigm shift is the natural order of things, its moment has arrived.

It is inevitable right now

We have finally reached the state in our evolution where there is an enormous number of enlightened people and that is changing our paradigm. We will step up and take control of our lives. And again, never for a minute think that just because you are not physically active in helping, that you are not having an effect. Your psychic participation has profound implications and will support the change that we are all working towards at this time.

This paradigm shift cannot be stopped.

So, keep the faith is what it boils down to

Expand your faith so that it encompasses all religions, all races and all things.

A global paradigm shift is happening at this very moment.

Actually thinking about a better world or better situation **is intention** and that intention inspires and **influences the infinite intelligence** to create a reality that supports that "will."

We the people want to be loved, want to be free, we want to have a world where there is security, peace and respect for everything. This is our right.

The Enlightened Age
This is big, this is global.
We are changing the way we understand
ourselves as beings

What a glorious age we are in! I am thrilled with this moment. The paradigm shift has begun. There are tens of millions of people soon running into the billions who are spiritually awakening. We will soon reach critical mass and in that moment an unstoppable flood of intention will usher us into a New Age.

The age of love, peace and harmony.

This is not a dream, this is fact.

The Family of Man

There are amazing things that are happening at this time. As we enter the age of spiritual enlightenment we open the door to miracles.

Other beings will seek us out and invite us to explore the stars, not as strangers but as family.

And our adventure continues…..

A Whisper

A whisper
Almost but not quite
I strain to hear
Is it a memory?
I believe so
But of what, of when?

It is a sweet memory
It lingers – but a moment
Then is gone

Yet
And yet
I know this whisper
It whispers of family
Of friends, of home

A whisper
From all those loved and lost
That have passed
And not passed
Aware and unaware alike

A whisper from the timeless
The formless
I will pursue this whisper
This soft calling
I will remember

Paul Manuel

We are Divine Beings

Remember

There is a light
At the end of the tunnel
There is a light
In the brilliance of your mind
There is a light
To soften the darkness
It will comfort
In the darkest of times

Just open
Your heart
To the angels
Your sisters
And brothers
On high
They are waiting
With love
To embrace you
You need only open your mind

It is true
That you
Are an angel
You have just forgotten
For a while

Paul Manuel

But it is time now
For you to awaken
It is time for you
To come back home

You have been lost
In the folds of corruption
Not your fault
Just illusions in time
Open your heart
To your angel
It is time for you
To come back home

We are waiting
Your sisters and brothers
It is time now
For you to recall
It is time now
For you to remember
It is time to remember
Who you are

You, are an angel
Time to awaken
It is time to come back
To the stars

Be Robbed Not

I have travelled far
And I tire

What path led
And leads?
This path called life

I journey without remorse;
Yet I would
That it were a more
Joyous pursuit

Stride forward
Says the sage
Fear not
Thy lot in life
Follow thy heart
Without reservation

But lo:
The journey

Black heart
The hustler
Companion untrue
Played my strings
Plucked to my rhythm
Sweet deceit

Paul Manuel

Through friend
Or noble spirit
My eyes were opened
Just in the nick
I was spared loss
And given gain
This wisdom in trust

Grudge not the thief
For in that
You have been robbed

Bear witness to the noble
Honor their intervention
With acceptance
And be robbed not

Hello

Hello!
Can you hear me?
Am I so insignificant
As to be ignored?

Am I silent in my appeal?
A whisper of despair
Better left ignored

Speak to me
I am your family
Do you not recognize my heart?
My smile, my need?

I am a seed
To be nurtured
To be cared for
To be loved
To grow healthy

Is it not so
That you are the same?
A seed to be nurtured
To be cared for
To be loved
To grow healthy?

Are we not one and the same?

Paul Manuel

We are divinity experiencing

unlimited potential

A Masterpiece

Evening sky
Red-rimmed clouds
Hung in softest blue
I cry in ecstasy
A longing deep inside
Emotions welling up
To crest in crystal tear

Oh evening sky
Sunset's song
Caressing memories of old
Bringing sweet
Forget-me-nots
To linger in repose

What joy caresses
Through my thoughts
Rolling head to toe
A sweet recall
Of love reclaimed
It matters not
Place or name
Just passion
Of the closing day
A soft display
Of parting's way

Paul Manuel

A 'bye for now
Until the morrow
Offers up again
To stir emotions
To claim the right
To open eyes
To see the light
Then fade
Into a velvet night
To depths of inner sight

To reflect upon
Without intent
Be one with all
Heaven sent

To be a masterpiece
Of song
To be a symphony
Then gone

But always to return

Last Breath

How sweet is this last breath
That has no rival
All of my memories unfolding
Reliving my life in this last breath

Ice melting, such a torrent
A stick boat
Disappearing into a culvert pipe
To appear a moment later
Continuing on its journey of adventure
Down the drain and gone
.....a living thing in my eyes
Bringing more joy than can be imagined

The slow wonderful explosion of spring
Running with my friends down the lane
Joyous in living

My poor weeping heart
The bully who abused me
Without fault
Something from their being abused

Swimming in the creek
Playing under the waterfall
Mom and Dad on a blanket watching
Their friends, my friends, together

Jumping into leaf piles
Could anything be more fun?
Innocence
The true wellspring of joy

Sliding down the hill at the park
Dad pulling us along on our toboggan
Mom on the toboggan holding us tight

Paul Manuel

Could anything be greater?

Slowly, suddenly
I sense self
In ways unknown
I become thoughtful
I experience the other
As unique

I somehow stand alone
With a deep need for companionship
Just before body electric
Starts and stops
Unsure
Ever forward
Friends searching together
Yet apart

Suddenly puppy love
Infatuation
Hormones running wild

A new door opens just a crack
A world presents
No going back
Amazing
To say the least
A roar of pent-up emotions
Unsure
But ever on

What a rush is this adventure
To careen through adolescence
To adult

Still in ways unsure
Ever seeking, understanding
Learning to accept in others
The failings I find
In me

Facing love
Not always true
But always somehow real
Not understanding love
Unclear on how I feel

Mating
A commitment
Children
A delight
Watching life unfold for them
Knowing things are right

Mature in understanding
Years comfortably slip by
At peace
In knowing harmony
From seeking to know why
Seeing the truth
Behind the mask
Living the here and now

My life unfolds
The good, the bad
Sorrow, pain, laughter

Together in this last breath
The nectar of a lifetime

Paul Manuel

We are in constant amazement,

joyous in being

My Conceit

A rip
In my conceit
By the plight
Of my fellow man
The rift between
Have and not
Our heads
Stuck in the sand

May the wind of time
Expose our sins
Shame
To shake our souls
Extend our hands
To our fellow man
If we don't
Our souls
We have sold

See beyond
The hate and fear
Hunger
Is their excuse
Caused by our indifference
We have allowed
Untold abuse

We are the constant being

Never Say Die

Blackstrap molasses
On a slab a' sourdough
A belt a' shine
Feelin fine
Lunch is over
I'm back in the mine

Deep underground
Mountain on my back
More crushing everyday

I came here for gold
I'd get rich quick
Back home
Done
Lickety split

Who's kidding who?
Been here two years
Clothes are all ragged
Cold, wet, dried up tears

Paul Manuel

Came here a young man
I'll be leaving old
My family's back home
At least they were
Haven't had mail
In over a year

I've had enough!
Can't take it no more
Leaving in the morning
I'm outa here!

Well, maybe

Just one more day
Just one more pick
Just one more shovel
Might strike it yet!

The Wind

What poem comes to mind
About the wind, a friend of mine
As daylight pushes back the night
I see the wind in all its might

Trees back-dropped by constant grey
Thrashing in the wind they play
Letting fly cone and bow
To revel in the here and now

The wind, it plays the song of life
High and low, drum and fife
Rat-a-tat-tat on tin roof play
The wind today, will have its way

Paul Manuel

Nothing does not exist

A Moment has Passed

A moment has passed
My life is drawing near
The experience of my lifetime
Every moment I hold dear

A reflection of my will to be
A doodle on the fabric of time
As fleeting as this moment has been
The moment has been mine

Some things I've done were ugly
Others were divine
I judge not what I have been
I was child that is all
I was child
I am child

I forgive and in that I find I judge
I have many contradictions
Is that sentient?
I guess

How sweet has been this journey
For the love I have received I am blessed
To love as deeply
As I have loved
Is my reward for being true
And forgiveness for my deceits

Humbled before God
Humbled before self
My ego is silenced

A moment has passed
My life is drawing near

The experience of my lifetime
Every moment
I hold dear

The Unnamed

Mountain among mountains
The deity of snow sits

Eons pass, to man
Yet undisturbed
Sits the unnamed
Content to observe

White crown cool and pristine
Draping its shoulders in glory

A shawl of love
Given by kindred cloud
Drifting unfettered
A changeling
No more, no less than any...

From time to time
A smudge of soot
From kindred earth
Bursts forth from inner furnace
To flash, to cool, to sleep
A moment, no more, no less

Paul Manuel

Wind – a rage – a whisper
A friend of long standing
Before water, before cloud
But a child – to Mother Earth
And the Unnamed

Life, a blanket of mix and mingle
A moment to root
A moment to cover
A moment to pass

Sun, old friend
Beloved to the Unnamed
Is also passing – again

The Unnamed
Drifting
Ever in awe
Ever thankful
Content to observe
Without expectation

The Glory of Creation

We are moving into an Enlightened Age

Fairy Flight

Fairies
Oh how I wish
For their return
My heart
Would swell with glee

I know they will
For I've been told
They will if I believe

Well as you see
I do believe
In castles
Fair and bright

I wait
With bated breath
To hear
The sound
Of fairy flight

Paul Manuel

The past is just memories

The future yet to be

Now is all there is, and will always be

The Way it Goes

Lurking in the recesses of my mind
Are demons
Of my own design
Clustered in quagmire thoughts
Oozing forth
Whispering strange suggestions
Giving no peace
Threatening to burst
Sending tendrils
Creeping through the rational
Twisting, knotting, mocking
Seeking to control

I've tried the mask
It didn't work
Heard sex would work
Didn't though
Tried most everything
To stop the flow
Damn it, damn it
It just won't go

Paul Manuel

Must step outside
To see its hold
So I'm told
But damn it all
I'm getting old
No quick fix
But then again
Forgiveness lies
Just within

I know, I know
I must let go
Simple when found
And there you go

Just step outside
The ego's hold
I wish I could have
Years ago
Could have stopped a lot of pain
I suppose
But you know what
That's just the way it goes

In the Moment

A princess bound by protocol
Gazed longingly in dream
To be a spirit
Free and pure
Without expectancy

The court
Left little room to be
To be
Oh just to be
Never a soul
So closely bound
None, so bound as she

A glance, by chance
The moment pure
In meadow
Forest bound
A shepherd boy
Apparently
By dress it would appear –
Lay next a boulder
Old and grey
From whence he came, unclear

The maiden princess
Longed to join
To walk the meadow fair
To sit and talk
To one at peace
The boy
That lingered there

Paul Manuel

The portal framed
A world apart
Forbidden
By decree
But how her heart
Yearned to be
As boy
In meadow, free

Against a boulder
Old and grey
A young man
Gypsy bred
Looked unto
The castle fair
And dreamed he there instead

His heartstrings hummed
A melody
Of joy and festival
Of pomp
And ceremony
The freedom there
To be

The life of day to day
Of shelter, food and drink
Was a point of rub
Unknown to those
In castle
Did he think

Oh to live
The pampered life
All one's needs be met
To live a life
Full and rich
A life without regret
To be a prince
In yonder bode
In castle
To be free

Their spirits touched
In common thought
Both knew
It could not be

Their spirits twinned
And danced in joy
In the moment
Both, were free

Paul Manuel

There is Wisdom in all things

The Mariner

Cradled
By the continents
Is a jewel
Most divine
Oh ocean
How I love thee
For you soothe my weary mind
You nurture me
You mend me
You free my very soul

My love for thee
Is boundless
I love thee
Pole to pole

When I die
Please send my ashes
Out upon the sea
And know
That I will rest in peace
For you
Have set me free

The Universe is Conscious of being

And we are that consciousness

Thankful

The caress of sunshine
Soft on my cheek
The sparkles it sends
From rippling creek

Inspires my heart
To revel in glory
Of every days blessings
Of every day's story

The infinite epic
The unfolding tale
Of heroes and heroines
Their exploits, to hail

Sunshine
Sunshine
Brings always to me
A great joy of living
It sets my soul free

And I say
From my heart
I am thankful
To be

A Speck of Mist

A speck of mist
Set adrift
Across the landscape fair
Beneath the moonlit
Starry night
It drifts
Without a care

To follow
Where its mates may go
To gather in a drop of dew
To bathe
In moonlight's silver hue

To sparkle
With the rising sun
To drift again
Till day is done
To mingle
Once again as dew
Again to bathe
In moonlight's
Silver hue

Paul Manuel

If you are searching for the awareness of your

complete identity

You have turned on the "light"

The Sun and the Wind

Where are all the fish my friend?
Just memories left
Of way back when

Where have all the great trees gone?
Not much left
All cut down

The sun still shines
The wind still blows
Over a landscape
Scraped for gold

Vast fishing fleets
Thousands strong
Is there any wonder
Things went wrong?

Old timers talking
Of times gone by
Cutting and falling
They still
Get a glint in their eye

The days of adventure
The power of youth
No one asked
That's the truth

Paul Manuel

The door was opened
No going back
Man against nature
Money
On a fast track

Nature suffered
Few complained
You know the saying
No pain, no gain

All gone now
But what a gas
What's done is done
The past is the past

But whoever thought
It would end so fast
But end it has
We can't pretend
Just memories left
Of way back when

Blessed

My child, my heart
Are as one
Newborn, looking into my eyes
A manifestation of the infinite truth

Innocent, fragile, beautiful
My being revels in serenity
Such as I have never known

What a joyous journey
We have now begun
To grow in ways
Neither of us could have imagined

Up all hours
Taking care of your every need
With gladness in my heart
Your needs are my needs
My love is boundless

As the years unfold
Stride forward
Strong and true to thyself

I am honored
To be part of your experience
And Blessed
That you, are a part of mine

Paul Manuel

The Universe is aware

and we are that awareness

The Being of Legend

Could anyone be
More beautiful than you?
You're at your best
Just being you

Strong, fragile
Aspire to the greater truth
My world
Is so much richer
Because of you

You're my sister
My brother
My daughter
My son
My mother
My father
The infinite one

You bring out the best
Your spirit is pure
You are child-like
With humor
In wisdom, mature

In essence
You are truth
Honest and pure
You're divine
You are the glory
You are the being of legend

All this you are
And so much more
Could anyone be
More beautiful
Than you?

Paul Manuel

This is an interactive experience

The Substance of Dreams

Into my thoughts
Soft cloud immersion
Gentle and peaceful
My life, a reunion

A flow of memories
Lift from the pool
Clear for my viewing
Focus
In the midst of the collage
Of my experience

To rest in the flavor
Of a chosen moment
To find forgiveness
In the recollection of regrets

Lost, at times
In a splash of recollection
A maelstrom of confusion
A profusion of emotion

As ambrosia
Ever welcome
A delight to the palate

The bitter, the sweet
The bittersweet

The substance of dreams

We are awakening , not from a dream

But metaphorically as in "Becoming Aware"

of our complete nature

Bounce Back

Where has it gone?
My lifetime's passed
In some ways it's true
Save the best for last

But looking back
Where is the line
I can't tell
Is that a crime?

There were many ups
Several downs
Life's like a circus
And I'm like a clown
I always bounce back
When I get knocked down

Yeah, the best for last
Is an unknown line
You could miss it waiting
Now that
Would be a crime

If you're lucky you're old
When you see the sign
But there is never a clock
With an ending time

So each day is your last
Until proven wrong
If you follow this rule
You can't go wrong

Paul Manuel

Every knock's a boost
Every day is your last
Cry a little
But it's best to laugh

Be kind and gentle
Have no regrets
Live for the moment
I mean
What the heck?

Don't judge too harshly
In fact
Try to judge not at all

And remember
Bounce back
Whenever you fall

As One

Close to my heart
You are my comfort
Naked before you
In body and soul
I am at ease

This being in time
With all of its flaws
Finds comfort in your presence
Your judgments are fast
And fleeting
Spoken, received
Then forgotten

I am exposed before you
Yet, you do not take advantage
An angel, a lover, a mate
No time for jealousy, anger or hate

Close to my heart?
Nay, a part of my heart
Now and always

Filled with sweet emotions
I drift forward through life
Strong and secure
We are soul mates you and I
Again nay, we are one another
In body and soul
We are the infinite being
Together, in love

Ship of Dreams

Staring off across the sea
Waiting for my ship of dreams
That will bring good things to me
My ship of dreams
My ship of dreams

Always waiting, for peace of mind
Leaving sorrow far behind
Never living here and now
But in my ship of dreams
Ever, in my ship of dreams

But my ship will come
At least I pray
Come and take me far away
Bring me peace
Oh happy day
My ship of dreams
My ship of dreams

Just beyond my mind's horizon
My ship of dreams
Is rising, rising
Always
Just beyond my grasp
My ship of dreams
My ship of dreams

Paul Manuel

Time my master
Marches on
Taking all
Leaving none
The carrot dangles, ever near
My ship of dreams
My ship of dreams

Never living in the now
Always living in the other
In memories
Of dreams soft lies
Or what will come
By and by
My ship of dreams
My ship of dreams

I tire of waiting
The cost too great

My ship is coming
Too late, too late!

My ship of dreams
My ship of dreams

I've lost my time;
In what might have been

The Constant Soldier: I Am War

A soldier tried and true
Sleeping one eye open
Finger on the trigger
I'm a soldier through and through
War is my game
And I like it like that

Been in the Boer War
I didn't give a damn
First, Second, Korea, Nam
Now I get it – I understand!
I have been killed many times
I just keep coming back
I'm a soldier
I like it like that

There's nothing like lead
In the back of the head
Puts ya out like a light
And mines – what a gas
They'll blow up your ass!
That's war
And I like it like that

I been gassed
I been slashed
I've been run over by a tank
That don't give ya much time to think
But I keep coming back
War after war
Yeah, I'm a soldier
And I like it like that

The deep concussion
Of canon fire
The roar of a Gatlin Gun
The thump of a mortar
Cordite smoke
Music on the run!

Hell
Yeah it's hell
But it's my hell
And I keep coming back
The world's in some kind of chaos
I'm a soldier
And I like it like that

If you keep on knocking
I'll open the door
A soldier by definition
Is a creature of war
Yeah it's ugly
And it's true
But who's keeping score
The rich stay rich
And the poor stay poor

Ya say ya don't like war
But ya keep me coming back
Yeah I'm a soldier
I am war
And I like it like that

This physical reality is a reality of

interaction

Opinion and judgment

With a less egoic approach we will make

much more intelligent decisions

Instead of knee-jerking along

We can make the decisions that will enhance

our experience in a harmonious fashion,

Where all things are realized as equal

Where respect and love are paramount

War is a Crime

War is the enemy of man
War is the enemy of man
Tell me what is the plan?
Tell me what is the reason?

War is the enemy of man
Can't you hear the cry?
War is a lie

War is the enemy of man
War after war
Tell me what is it for?
War is the enemy of man

War is the enemy
War is the enemy
War is the enemy of man

Time after time war is a crime
War is a crime
War is a crime

War is the enemy of man

War

War: it has no conscience
War: it doesn't listen
War: it happens when we pray
War: is here to stay

War: is a knee-jerk reaction
War: is planned by some for gain
War: it doesn't have compassion
War: is a beast of pain

War: lingers in our memory
War: belongs to the insane
War: is not for faint of heart
War: is a dirty game

War: is the child of obsession
War: can never fill its gut
War: is anger always wanting
War: is hatred on the hunt

War: will end when all is taken
War: will rage till nothing's left
War: is the beast of our destruction
War: will never let us rest

Paul Manuel

Caustic Bliss

I have sung the battle song
Weapon in hand
Killed from dawn till dusk
It matters not why
I must fight or die
It's all the same
Truth or lie

Death from axe, bullet or bomb
What matter the instrument
It plays but one song
Death

The tension before the storm
Soft quiet foreboding
Rattling nerves
Cascading thoughts
Silence

Slowly the rustle of dry leaf
The leading edge
Of the wind of death
A rising crescendo of fear
Lost in the moment
Cymbal, drum
String, horn, choir
War cry of the ages beyond care

Forward, forward is all
No hate, no fear, just death
Kill or be killed
Lost in the symphony
Of war

Paul Manuel

The trailing edge of conflict
Moans, groans, screams
Isolated weapon sound
Out of sync
From dying hand
Then silence

Silence most profound
The roaring silence
Of the battle ground
Peace not lost
Not found
Not sought
Just silence
No thought
The caustic bliss
Of war

Whispers of War

Whispers of war
Glorifying war
What waste

Bronze memories of war
Old riddled with scars
Of war after war

Forgotten pain and suffering
Bronze glory
Always hiding truth
Never learning from the past
Remembering only glory
In bronze

No blood, no pain in bronze
Just hidden memory
Just message disguised
The image of glory
In bronze

Win or lose
Monument to glory in bronze
Ever condoning
Through Illusion
Aggression

Lest we forget
But alas
We have forgotten
Again and again and again
Brothers and sisters
Waging war
Against brother and sister

Paul Manuel

Seeing only the beauty
Of bronze memories
Not the cauldron
Of blood, hate and fear
From which poured
The bronze memory of Glory

Awaken, Awaken
We have been mesmerized
No glory in bronze
Just lies
Just lies disguising
The memories of war
Disguising
The whispers of war
Disguised
In bronze

I have Learned Pain

I have learned pain
I have learned gain
I have soared high above

I have touched upon the answer
And turned back in my despair
I have tasted of compassion
I have seen it trampled under foot

I have seen anger turn to laughter
As the mob ran amuck

I have smoked the pipe of peace
I have drunk the wine of joy

I have stumbled in oblivion
I have dropped on knees in shame

I have seen my soul in kindred eye
I have trapped my soul in stone

I have sat on log in forest fair
I have sat on throne without a care

I have seen the light in fellow man
I have seen a vacant stare

Paul Manuel

It

It's a strange creature
It gets what it wants
The cost is unimportant
It's always on the hunt

It takes, takes, takes
It's never satisfied
What is the difference
In the end
It's only going to die

Who can blame it anyway
It knows not right from wrong
It really doesn't get it
Too busy having fun

At least it thinks it is
It's always me, me, me
Nature is on the run
Too bad
It won't stop
It must be free

It cries, cries, cries
What ever will it do?
The end is near
The picture clear
But all it does is chew

It just can't bring itself
To give up what it owns
It worked damned hard to get it
It is it's and it's alone
It is it's alright, that's for sure

It knows it in its bones
Such an it as it is
Will never leave it's throne

Paul Manuel

Go to War my Child

Time to go to war my child
I've given everything
There is nothing left to give
I have nothing left to spend

I have raised
And loved you tenderly
It's time you paid your dues
I didn't waste all these years
For you to sit and muse
About a better time to come
When everyone can choose
Whether or not to fight in wars
Now get off your ass
Move!

It's time to take action
I don't want to hear your blues
The bills are mounting up
I fear
I've way too much to lose

War is here
To put things right
Stand tall
Get in gear
Your eighteen now
Be a man
Wipe away that tear

Paul Manuel

Die
Or come back half a man
Just fight
You're young, you're strong
Get mean
It doesn't matter how you feel
It's the sacred war machine

God decided long ago
You should know what I mean
Go forth and conquer evil
Well we're broke
Times are lean

Forward child
What will be, will be
Honor will follow you
Fight
For God and country
I'll be waiting
When you're through

But if you're lost
On the battle field
Or come back in a body bag
Never forget
I love you my child
For you will have died
For what I believe

To Follow the Wind

Life is like a leaf
Blowing in the wind
Following the wind
Trusting the wind
Then caught in a tangle
Quivering, shaking, pulling
To be free

A sudden gust
And onward again
Rising to the sky
Without effort
Suddenly, caught in a whirlwind
Circling ever faster
Delight in abandon

The flow and ebb of experience
Rain to settle one to the earth
To lie in comfort of misty morn
Draped in crystal dew

Slowly, gracefully melding
As one with all
To mingle in the firmament
To taste eternity
To be at peace
To follow the wind

Paul Manuel

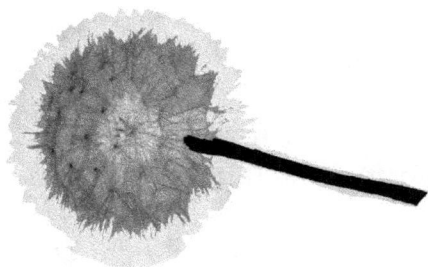

The Passing of Grief

To describe my grief is to say
That it is profound
Deep within my being
My foundation bleeds
Waves of sorrow cascade
Bursting through my heart
Unstoppable at times
At times held back
Straining emptiness

I hold in this grief
For fear of losing self
Like a storm within my breast
Screaming
To be free
To abandon this flood of emotion
Is not possible
It may drive me into the abyss
Of forgetfulness
Peace, yes
But to relinquish self
The price too great

I stand before the gate of myth
With others
In this pit of despair
With others
Alone
Yet together
All must stand before the gate of myth
With torn heart

Paul Manuel

Speak not wisdom here
It has no place
There is no understanding
There is but one comfort
To surrender
To this deluge
But I cannot
I will be swept into vortices
Of the unbearable

I fear, I rage, I weep
I sleep
But frightfully so
I know this grief is not mine alone
Yet it is my focus
In each and everyone

I would run, walk, fly
To escape
But it is without place
This grief
I must face what I cannot
Bear the unbearable
And pray

All this is but the chatter of anguish
I will survive
And be stronger
For the passing of grief
Is the presence of God
It is profound in its purity
Not unlike death
It reveals divinity

In its passing
I touch eternity
In sorrow
I awaken
I am humbled by this emotion

I touch God
And I am thankful
For what is grief but love's yearning
I have been blessed
I have loved
I have been loved
I have tasted the bittersweet
I stand before the door of myth without fear
Heart in hand
In silence
I weep

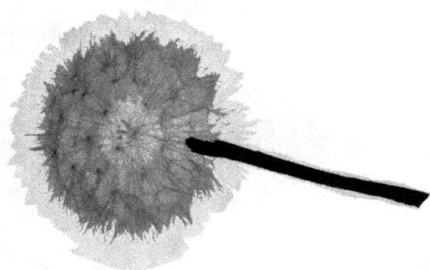

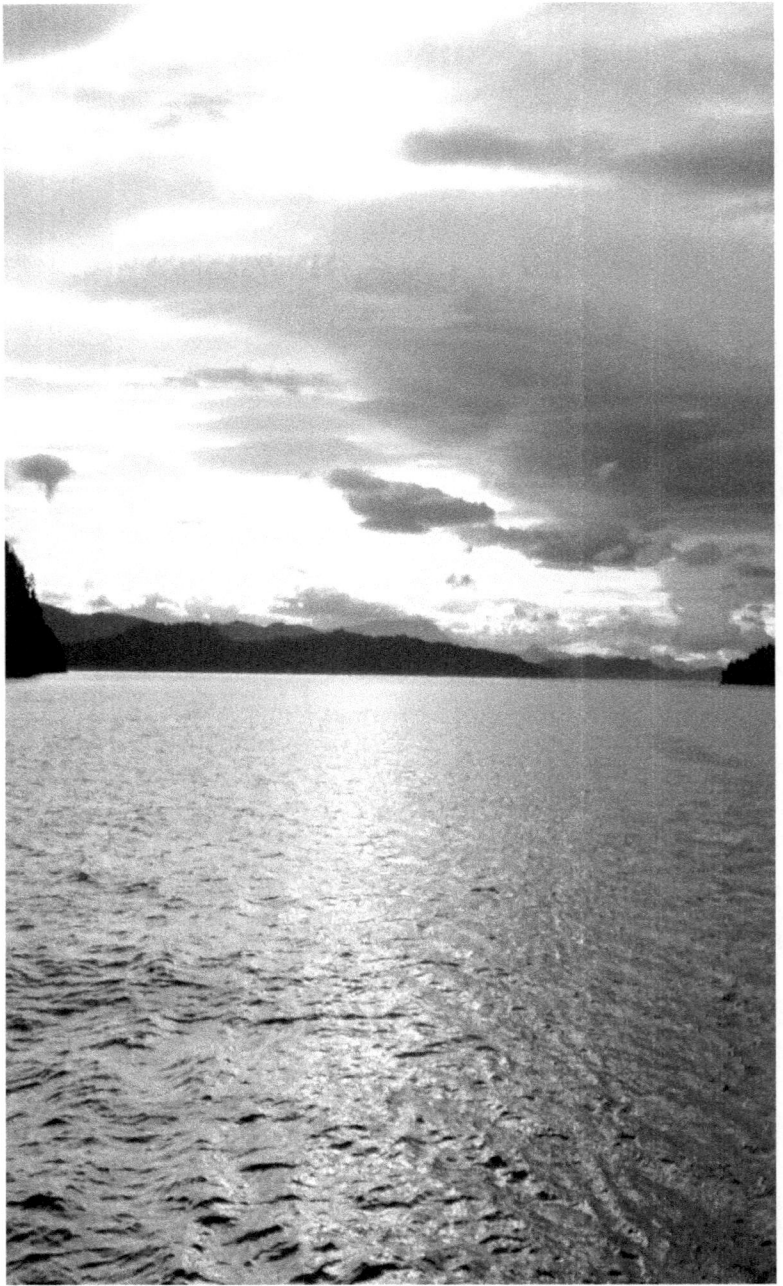

Salt Water Trail

Sail away my friend
Fight another day
Be at peace sailing
Embrace the wind and spray

Be at peace with nature
Joyful just in being
Stand before the mast my friend
You're on the salt water trail

A Book

A book of little nothings
Just thoughts in random prose
The fragrance of a wild rose
Caressing the confines of the close

Memories of those loved
Gently drifting through my mind
As I sit before the flickering fire
Cradled in my easy chair
A sweet chocolate drink to my lips

Jack Frost nipping at the door
Painting crystal pictures on the window panes
The distant calling of a train
Flooding memories of days gone by

Sweet sorrow swelling my breast
Of loves lost for the moment
At peace
Candlelight caressing my eyes
My spirit flies
But not too far
Beyond the confines of my room

Warm and toasty at ease
In the now and memories
Of days gone by

Paul Manuel

We are infinite eternal beings manifested

Within the parameters of time and space

Experiencing possibilities

Extinct

You may laugh
At the name you gave me
You may laugh at the way I looked
But you can only know about me
By reading a zoological book

I was happy and content
Without worry I went
Until you came along
Then my future was spent

In a moment it seems I was gone
It certainly didn't take very long
You can search all you want
You won't find me
You wouldn't let up now I'm gone

What on earth were you thinking?
I guess you weren't thinking at all
Just a knee-jerk reaction
You were hungry, I was food
That is all

There is no blame
Though it matters
And I'm sure there were those that cared
But we weren't the first to have fallen
Nor the last
In spite of their care

That aside
Your world was richer
Richer
When we were there

Paul Manuel

You may laugh
At the name you gave me
And you may laugh at the way I looked
But you can only know about me
By reading a zoological book

You called me a "Dodo" a no brainer
You felt good you chuckled inside
We trusted and that was our downfall
We trusted
And then we all died

You called me a "Dodo" it was easy
Dumb as a bump some would say
But I was happy
Content with my freedom
I looked forward to each coming day

Yes you may laugh
At the name you gave me
You may laugh
At the way I looked
But you can only know about me
By reading a zoological book

Daisy Petal Dream

It is a Daisy Petal Dream
He loves me, she loves me not
Early morning meadow
Alive with dew-clad webs
Glistening and sparkling
With rainbow hue
In the soft morning breeze
Beckoning imagination
Emotions without frame
What name have I
Amidst such as this?

I am the Daisy and the Dew
And the Web
My heart resonates
With sweet yearning
Swelling my breast
I am home
Not in words
But as foam
Upon a boundless sea
With divine understanding
Just Being

Words can only touch
What cannot be explained
This is all I have to offer
'Tis a Daisy Petal Dream

Poetry of Poverty

What is the poetry of poverty?
But misery and strife
The anguish of no escape

To trudge towards the light
A flickering candle
In a forest of sorrow
The only hope is God
Belief against all odds

A better world is waiting
Lord but why
The children
The children
I cry
Is there no mercy?
No compassion?

Is poverty to enslave?
A malignant force
Ending with the grave
The rhythm of tears
Pouring from kindred eye

Is poetry to enlighten?
To strike a chord of guilt
In our hearts
Is this
The poetry of poverty?

Paul Manuel

The universal manifestation aspect of our

reality responds to desire

It will respond to the energy not the content

Broken

I feel broken
In so many ways
I feel broken
What else can I say?
Something inside sizzles
Fizzles, dies
Yet lingers on as pain
I feel broken
In so many ways

Fear of future
Fear of past
Fear of loneliness
Fear of fear
I feel broken
In so many ways

Stresses, stretching
Churning gut
Seeking, shunning
Afraid to touch
Overwhelmed
I feel broken
In so many ways

Yet deep inside
Just beneath
I sense the place
Of inner peace

Paul Manuel

No judgments there
From being judged
No need to hide
Just Love, Just Love

Then burning shards
Splintered thoughts
Heavy clouds again
Lost in silent pain
I have no say
I only pray
I feel broken
In so many ways

Yet just beneath the surface
I sense the place of inner peace
No judgments there
From being judged
No need to hide
Just Love
And Peace
And Truth
I am illusions lost
I can see now
I Am Free

Love in Ecuador

You are a bouquet of flowers
You are a Sunday afternoon
You are a lazy rainy day
Nothing I'd rather do
Just chilling out with you

You are a wishing well
Fairy Dust
A stroll in a meadow by a stream
A carriage ride through Paris
On a warm summer eve
Sitting by a moonlit canal
A glass of fine red wine

An English country garden
A prairie harvest moon
Machu Picchu, the Nazca Plains
A mystery, the unexplained
An ocean sunset
A raging sea
All this you are to me

A starry night
The inner light
Galaxies and more
Music, friends, laughter
Sorrow, grief and tears
A picnic by the Tomebamba
Love in Ecuador

Paul Manuel

The Spider Waits

Speak to me Ecuador
Tell me of your passion
Speak to me in song
Show it in movement
Do not lose yourself
Your spirit
In the things of man

The net has been cast
Take what you need
Not what you covet
Many things come your way
In a flood of deceit
Desire is the seed
Greed is the emotion triggered
A great flood is coming
Take heed

For every flower
There grows a thousand weeds
Know your garden well
Don't buy into the game
Family, friends, community
Is the stake
Be careful of the web
The Spider Waits

Paul Manuel

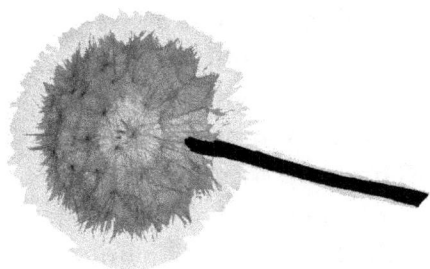

It is Time

What can I do to help?
When despair seems to reign supreme
Can anything I do make a difference?
Can anything possibly reduce the pain?
Can I pierce the cloud of misery?
It's a hard rain, it's a hard rain
Wherefore art thou Juliet?
Is love lost, are we forsaken?

In the act of asking, something stirs
Ripples in the pond, lady of the lake
Awaken, Awaken
The life line dangles
We need only grasp
All is not lost Horatio
There are strange things done
Under the midnight sun
In the face of overwhelming odds

Onward, onward, into the fray
Whispering sweet forget-me-nots
We are free, we are free
Blessed are the meek
The righteous hand in hand
Shall overcome all obstacles
Faith shall mountains move
The Dickens I say
We shall overcome
We shall overcome

Paul Manuel

The fabled rock and a hard place
The ever elusive door
The Pearly Gates
Muhammad's Mount
The Buddha state
The rabbit's watch
I'm late, I'm late

The Kings and Queens
Have gathered in the sheaves
The harvesters blowing in the wind
Like fallen leaves
Yet where but from the compost
Springs the greenest of the green

A new world is waiting
Says the sage
Rosemary and Thyme
A feast for all, for all
A feast of peace and harmony
For all
'Tis not a battle cry
Fall back, Fall back
No, ever on, ever on
A magic carpet ride
Once upon a time is lost
A story told in rhyme
Ever on, ever on
It is time, it is time

About the Author

Paul was born in New Brunswick Canada in 1947. When he was quite young his family moved to Ontario, just outside of Toronto. They lived in a cottage in a valley by a beautiful river.

He was raised in a bit of both worlds, sort of downtown country folk.

He left home when he was sixteen, traveling to Vancouver BC. A Gypsy at heart he has continued to travel throughout his life. He moved to Vancouver Island in 1978 and eventually settled in the Cowichan Valley which has been his home base for 22 years.

Over the years he has developed into a singer/songwriter and poet. His writings utilize humor, whimsy and philosophy, all intended to inspire.

We are infinite beings experiencing physical reality.

To realize this truth, we must view this reality from our divinity state.

www.ingramcontent.com/pod-product-compliance
Lightning Source LLC
Chambersburg PA
CBHW072007040426
42447CB00009B/1528